WITHDRAWN

Dylan Thomas

by G. S. FRASER

Published for the British Council
and the National Book League
by Longmans, Green & Co

Three shillings and sixpence net

When Dylan Thomas died in New York in 1953 he was at the height of his fame. His *Collected Poems* had already enjoyed great success and he had shown exceptional gifts as broadcaster, entertainer, conversationalist and story-teller. Since his death, argument about his work has continued, and the current response to *Under Milk Wood* shows how alive general interest remains. This affectionate portrayal of life in a Welsh village, originally written for broadcasting, has enjoyed wide success on stage and television.

Mr G. S. Fraser, who will be remembered particularly for his study of W. B. Yeats in this Series, has written a highly personal study of Dylan Thomas's poetry. It will be of value to all who wish both to understand his impact on contemporaries and to assess his place in literature.

NOTE. *Thanks are tendered to Dylan Thomas's publishers, Messrs J. M. Dent & Sons, and his literary agents, Messrs. Higham (David) Associates Ltd for kind permission to quote extensively from his work.*

DYLAN THOMAS
from a portrait by AUGUSTUS JOHN
National Museum of Wales

DYLAN THOMAS

by

G. S. FRASER

PUBLISHED FOR
THE BRITISH COUNCIL
AND THE NATIONAL BOOK LEAGUE
BY LONGMANS, GREEN & CO

LONGMANS, GREEN & CO LTD
Longman House, Burnt Mill, Harlow, Essex

*Associated companies, branches and
representatives throughout the world*

*First published 1957
Reprinted 1960
Revised 1964
Reprinted with additions to bibliography 1969*
© G. S. Fraser, 1957, 1964

*Printed in Great Britain by
F. Mildner & Sons, London, EC1*

DYLAN THOMAS

I. INTRODUCTION

WHEN DYLAN THOMAS died in New York in his thirty-ninth year at the end of 1953, he had been a poet of considerable reputation for twenty years and, with the recent publication of his *Collected Poems*, was at the height of his fame. The collected volume was known to have sold, even before his death, more than ten thousand copies, an enormous figure by contemporary English or American standards. He was one of the two or three poets of his time whose name, like that of Mr Eliot or Mr Auden, was familiar to the man in the street. Shortly after his death, the success over the air and on the stage of his dramatic prose fantasy for radio, *Under Milk Wood*, introduced his work to an even wider audience than that which appreciated his poetry. It was not only, however, as a writer that Thomas was known to a wide public. He had a remarkable gift as an entertainer, and was a first-rate broadcaster, particularly of his own short stories based on his childhood in Wales. He was an extremely gregarious man, and had a very warm and lovable personality. His death produced a spate of tributes in prose and verse from scores of friends and acquaintances. And even for those who did not know him personally, Thomas had become, as few poets of our age have become, a kind of legend. He corresponded, as most poets do not, to some popular ideal, vision, or fiction of what a poet, in real life, should be. He was the pattern of the poet as a bohemian, and this was in many ways a misfortune for him. Had he been a more aloof, a less gregarious, a more prudent man; had he been less ready to expend himself in casual sociability; had he had less of a knack, in his later years, for earning money quickly and spending it even more quickly: in any of these cases, he might have lived longer and produced more; but he would not have been, in any of these cases, the writer that he is.

Thomas achieved, and has retained, a popular fame as a poet in spite of the fact that many of his poems are, at least on an intellectual level, extremely hard to comprehend. The design of at any rate many of his earlier poems is notably obscure; many of his later poems are much clearer in outline than his earlier work, but they are still full of puzzling details. Yet he is one of the few modern poets who can be read aloud to a large, mixed audience, with a confidence in his 'going down'. There is a massive emotional directness in his poems that at once comes across. And the more critical reader, who may be suspicious of what seems a direct attack on his feelings below the level of the intellect, soon becomes aware that Thomas's obscurity is not that of a loose and vague but of an extremely packed writer. In one of the best short studies that have been written of Thomas since his death, Dr David Daiches quotes what is certainly, at a first glance, an almost totally opaque passage:

> Altarwise by owl-light in the halfway house
> The gentleman lay graveward with his furies;
> Abaddon in the hangnail cracked from Adam,
> And, from his fork, a dog among the fairies,
> Bit out the mandrake with tomorrow's scream. . . .

Dr Daiches comments:

The careful explicator will be able to produce informative glosses on each of these phrases, but the fact remains that the poem is congested with its metaphors, and the reader is left with a feeling of oppression. . . . But it must be emphasized that this is not the fault of a bad romantic poetry, too loose and exclamatory, but comes from what can perhaps be called the classical vice of attempting to press too much into too little space.

In spite of this excessive congestion of much of his poetry, Thomas obviously did succeed in communicating in verse, to a very large public by modern standards, something which that public felt to be important. What was that something, and how did Thomas get it across? It was certainly something very different from the public personality, the personality of an entertainer, which Thomas conveyed in a prose book, *Portrait of the Artist as a Young Dog*. Thomas was not, like Byron or Yeats, for instance, the poet as actor; he did not dramatize his personal life in his poetry, or build himself up as a 'character'. He did these things in conversation, and in the sketches and short stories, brilliant improvisations, which were fundamentally an extension of his genius for conversation. His poems are exceedingly individual, but they are also impersonal; when he writes about his childhood he is not so much recalling particular experiences as transforming them into a vision of innocence before the Fall. Yet at the same time, he is a concrete rather than a generalizing poet; he does not, like Mr Auden, take a more or less abstract theme and proceed to relate it, in a detached way, to particularized observations about man and society. Both the appeal and the difficulty of his poetry come from the fact that it is a poetry of unitary response. Many of the best modern writers have been concerned with a kind of split in the consciousness of our time between what men think and what they feel or would like to feel, between what men suppose to be true and what they would like to believe, between what men feel is a proper course of action and what they feel is an attractive one. These urgent contemporary themes of stress, doubt, division in the self, tragic irony and tragic choice, do not enter into Dylan Thomas's poetic world. It is a world quite at one with itself. At the heart of his poetic response to experience there is a baffling simplicity.

II. LIFE, PERSONALITY AND PROSE

It is Thomas's poetry that makes him important and, because of this baffling simplicity at the heart of it, his personal history, outside the history of his poems, can perhaps throw very little direct light on his achievements as a poet. His prose works, with the exception of *Under Milk Wood*, also throw little light on his poetry. They are second-level

achievements, representing Thomas as the brilliant entertainer rather than the dedicated poet; they stand also, as so
much of Thomas's personal life did, for that search for dis-
traction which the concentrated nature of his dedication to
poetry made necessary. Thomas's poetry is the main theme
of this essay, but I shall precede my consideration of it by a
few brief remarks on Thomas's life, his personality, and his
achievements in prose.

Thomas was the son of a Swansea schoolmaster, a teacher
of English in a grammar school, who had himself poetic
ambitions; Thomas's father must have had remarkable gifts
as a teacher, for many of the leading figures today in Welsh
literary life were, at one time or another, his pupils. The
Welsh, like the Scots, have a very strong family sense, and
in his later years memories of holidays with farmer uncles
meant a great deal to Thomas. He was not a particularly
brilliant schoolboy, but he did very well at English, took an
enthusiastic part in amateur dramatics, and wrote neat and
very conventional poems for his school magazine. His father
would have liked him to work hard to gain a scholarship to
a university, but he did not do so. On leaving school,
he became for a short time a reporter on a Swansea newspaper, a job which must have combined for him the
appeal of bohemianism with that of the outer verges of
literature.

Thomas's Welshness is an important part of his make-up.
He never spoke or understood the Welsh language, and he
very early taught himself to speak English not with the
slight Welsh sing-song but with what he himself described
mockingly as a 'cut-glass accent'. He disliked Welsh
nationalism, and, indeed, all types of nationalism, but Wales
remained to him home. His knowledge of the Bible, and his
fundamentally religious—emotionally rather than intellec-
tually religious—attitude to life were typically Welsh; his
bohemianism was partly a reaction against the severe
puritanism of much of middle-class Welsh life. His sense of
verbal music, his feeling for the intricate interplay of vowel

and consonant, and also, in prose and conversation, his love of the extravagant phrase and the witty exaggeration were Welsh. He was un-English also in his universal gregarious-ness, his unwillingness to make social discriminations, his complete lack of class-consciousness.

He first became known as a poet through contributing poems to, and winning prizes from, the poetry page of the *Sunday Referee*, edited by Victor Neuberg. The *Sunday Referee* finally financed the publication of his first volume, *Eighteen Poems*. Thomas was thus flung on the London literary world, particularly its bohemian side, as a boy of twenty, and in his early years in London he depended a great deal on the generosity and hospitality of friends. In his later years, however, his wide range of secondary gifts, as a broadcaster, a writer of sketches and short stories and film scripts, even as a comic journalist, were bringing him in a considerable yearly income; this tended, however, to be spent as soon as it was earned, and his payment of income tax was perpetually overdue. He lost, in later years, his taste for London life, and spent as much time as he could with his wife and children at Laugharne. It was monetary need that drove him to undertake the American poetry-reading tours, which both he and those who organized them found a con-siderable strain as well as a stimulus, and on the last of which he died. Mr John Malcolm Brinnin's book about these tours is obviously almost agonizingly accurate in its descrip-tions of many embarrassing episodes, but it is a portrait of a sick man under the strain of financial and moral worry, and of being perpetually on public show, and it should not be taken as giving a fair idea of the character or personality of Dylan Thomas as his English friends knew him. In particu-lar it conveys a vivid impression of the element of stress, but no impression at all of the element of fulfilment, in Thomas's married life; Mr Brinnin's remarks about this should be corrected by Roy Campbell's that Thomas and his wife were 'always in love, even years after marriage to the day of his death. They would quarrel like newly-weds on the slightest

pretext with never a dull moment and make it up in two
minutes'.

In America, Thomas tended to drink whisky rather than
beer, though he knew spirits were bad for him. In England
and Wales, he stuck on the whole to beer, not for its own
sake, but as what his friend Vernon Watkins called 'a
necessary adjunct to conversation'. The tempo of his English
life was slower, more genial, and less harassed than that of his
tours in America. The charm of his rambling, vivid, extra-
vagantly anecdotal conversation comes out in *Portrait of the
Artist as a Young Dog* and in many of his broadcast sketches.
The warmth of his personality, his zest in every kind of
human oddity, his love for his fellow men, comes out in his
last completed work, *Under Milk Wood*. Here, more than in
any other prose work of his, he managed to combine his
prose gift for humorous fantasy based on realistic observa-
tion with his poetic gift for a piled-up richness of evocative
language. *Under Milk Wood* is also, purely formally, notable
as an invention. It derives not from any literary model, but
from the radio form of the 'feature', in narrative and dialogue, evoking the spirit of a place; it turns that form into
literature. It also makes more broadly and obviously
apprehensible than, perhaps, any of Thomas's poems do
that 'love of Man and . . . praise of God' which, in the introduction to the *Collected Poems*, Thomas wrote of as under-
lying all his work. *Under Milk Wood* is not, in the ordinary
sense, dramatic. The characters are not confronted with
choices; they behave according to their natures, mean,
thriftless, or generous, and are to be accepted, like natural
objects, for being what they are; and the movement is not
dramatic, but cyclical, from early morning through day to
night.

There are perhaps two moral centres in *Under Milk Wood*:
the Reverend Eli Jenkins, with his touching 'good-bad'
poems and his gentle appeals to a gentle God to look kindly
on human failings; and the old blind sea-captain, the fire of
whose lust and love—it is typical of Thomas's unitary

response to refuse to distinguish between these—is not quenched even by the waters of death and of utter forgetfulness. Thomas was as a man, like the Reverend Eli Jenkins, utterly without malice. Reading *Under Milk Wood* it is possible to understand what a famous newspaper, in a remarkable obituary notice of Thomas, meant by asserting that he had the courage to lead the Christian life in public. 'The harlots and the publicans shall go into heaven before you.'

III. *EIGHTEEN POEMS*

In an early statement about his poems, published in Mr Geoffrey Grigson's poetry periodical of the 1930s, *New Verse*, Thomas spoke of the process of writing a poem as one of stripping away darkness, of struggling up to light; and also of that struggle as taking place through a dialectic of images. In his preface to his *Collected Poems*, on the other hand, he spoke, as we have seen, of his poems being written 'for the love of Man and in praise of God'. These two statements help us to measure a certain progress, or development, in a poetic achievement which is too often thought of as having been one of more or less stationary self-repetition. In many of his early poems, Thomas does, in fact, seem immersed, in a way that is bewildering to the reader and may have been bewildering to himself, in an attempt to grasp the whole of life, human and natural, as an apparently confused but ultimately single process. In his later poems, he more often seems to be, quite consciously and much less bewilderingly, *celebrating* that process—celebrating it, as Dr Daiches says, religiously, and with sacramental imagery.

Perhaps also it is wrong to speak of him as celebrating some particular process; an American critic has suggested that what Thomas can be thought of as celebrating is the fact, or notion, of process in general, Eliot's 'three things', 'birth, and copulation, and death', seeing them as cyclical, seeing every birth as involving death, every death as involving birth, seeing also human life and natural process as exactly equated.

Such a set of clues certainly helps us a good deal with Thomas's earlier poems:

> The force that through the green fuse drives the flower
> Drives my green age; that blasts the roots of trees
> Is my destroyer.
> And I am dumb to tell the crooked rose
> My youth is bent by the same wintry fever . . .

Thomas, there, is massively identifying the body of man with the body of the world. The forces, he is saying, that control the growth and decay, the beauty and terror of human life are not merely similar to, but are the very same forces as we see at work in outer nature. But how is Thomas able to hold and move us by saying this? In a way, it is a platitude: it is a statement, at least, which most of us would accept without too much excitement or perturbation up to a point, or with qualifications. Man, as an animal, is part of nature; is that a new or startling idea? My own answer, when many years ago I first considered the puzzle of the extremely powerful impact of this passage, was this. The man-nature equation here gains strength from an inter-transference of qualities between—or, more strictly, of our emotional attitudes towards—man and nature. We feel a human pity for Thomas's 'crooked rose', and, on the other hand, the 'wintry fever' of an adolescent's unsatisfied sexual desires acquires something of the impersonal dignity of a natural process.

It is still, I think, the best clue that we have at least to Thomas's earliest volume, *Eighteen Poems*, to think of him as engaged in this way in bestowing on something humanly undignified, adolescent frustration, natural dignity:

> I see you boys of summer in your ruin.
> Man in his maggot's barren.
> And boys are full and foreign in the pouch.

I am the man your father was.
We are the sons of flint and pitch.
O see the poles are kissing as they cross.

The American critic, Mr Elder Olson, interprets the
whole poem from which this stanza comes—the first poem
in Dylan Thomas's first book—as a dialogue between per-
verse youth and crabbed age, with the poet occasionally
intervening as an impersonal commentator. Mr Olson's
ingenuity leaves out, however, the most obvious thing.
The poem is not only *about* the boys of summer in their
ruin, but *by* one of them. It seeks to give oratorical emphasis
and nobility of gesture to a subject which literature can
usually touch on only furtively or with condescending pity
—the subject of the sexual frustrations suffered by, and also
the agonizingly intense erotic imaginings that obsess, in an
advanced and therefore in many ways repressive civilization
like our own, the middle-class adolescent male. Thomas
began to write his poems in his late 'teens. It is in his late
'teens that the sexual desires of the male are at their most
urgent, and that his sexual potency is at his greatest; it is in
his late 'teens also, in our society, that he has least chance of
satisfying or exercising one or the other in a normal fashion.
What Thomas is doing in many of his earliest poems is find-
ing poetic symbols adequate to this experience, which is
centrally important in most masculine life-histories, but
which it is difficult to treat not only with literary, but even
with ordinary, decency. He also expresses the wider sense of
traumatic shock, a shock at once of awe and horror, which is
likely to accompany, for any young male in our civilization,
the full imaginative realization of 'the facts of life'. He went
on to do things more broadly significant than this; but this,
in itself, was a significant achievement.

IV. *TWENTY-FIVE POEMS*

Thomas's second volume, *Twenty-five Poems*, brought him
on the whole more praise and more fame than his first.
Dame Edith Sitwell, in particular, saluted it with enthusiasm
in a memorable short review in the *Observer*. Yet like many
second volumes of verse—and like all second novels!—
Twenty-five Poems is in many ways unsatisfactory. It shows
Thomas experimenting with new themes, new images, new
styles. Two poems in the book have, indeed, been much
praised, but to me it seems undeservedly. One is 'And
Death Shall Have No Dominion', which strikes me as a set
of large but rather empty rhetorical gestures, a poem in
which the poet faced by the harsh fact of death is not
properly confronting it but 'cheering himself up'. The other
is Thomas's one political poem, 'The Hand That Signed the
Paper'. That ends with this stanza:

> The five kings count the dead but do not soften
> The crusted wound nor stroke the brow;
> A hand rules pity as a hand rules heaven;
> Hands have no tears to flow.

That stanza has been praised as an example of a poet
splendidly and successfully mixing metaphors; may not
some, with all respect, find it rather an example of bathos?
There are other poems in *Twenty-five Poems* like 'Should
Lanterns Shine', which show us that Thomas had been
reading both Rilke, probably in translation, and Yeats:

> And from her lips the faded pigments fall,
> The mummy cloths expose an ancient breast . . .

> I have heard many years of telling,
> And many years should see some change.

> The ball I threw while playing in the park
> Has not yet reached the ground.

Such lines show a minor good taste in a composite manner

which is essentially *not* Thomas's. He had become, in his second volume, much more uncertain about the way he was going than in his first, and there is one poem which expresses his doubts admirably. Was, perhaps, his poetic method a method of self-deception?

> I have longed to move away
> From the hissing of the spent lie
> And the old terrors' continual cry
> Growing more terrible as the day
> Goes over the hill into the deep sea;
> I have longed to move away
> From the repetition of salutes,
> For there are ghosts in the air
> And ghostly echoes on paper,
> And the thunder of calls and notes.
>
> I have longed to move away but am afraid;
> Some life, yet unspent, might explode
> Out of the old lie burning on the ground,
> And, crackling into the air, leave me half-blind.
> Neither by night's ancient fear,
> The parting of hat from hair,
> Pursed lips at the receiver,
> Shall I fall to death's feather.
> By these I would not care to die,
> Half convention and half lie.

Thomas very rarely uses in his poetry the wit and humour of his personal conversation and his narrative prose. But here he manages to evade deep fears by mocking at shallow fears: '. . . night's ancient fear,/The parting of hat from hair' is simply a grotesque image of a man's being so frightened that his hair stands on end and pushes his hat off: as in a comic drawing by such a cartoonist as H. M. Bateman. The 'receiver' is simply a telephone receiver, and the poet's lips are 'pursed', as in a melodrama, because he is receiving a horrifying message. 'Death's feather' has no deep, obscure symbolic meaning but is simply an allusion to the humorous Cockney phrase: 'You could 'ave knocked me down with a feather!' (That, I think, is its use here; but it is quite a favourite phrase of Thomas's, and what he has often in mind is the custom of holding a feather to a dead man's lips to make sure he is no longer breathing.) These thrillerish fears, or self-induced, half-pleasant shudders, are 'half convention and half lie'. Neither the poetic imagination, nor sane, practical common sense, can afford to pay much attention to them. But the spent lie from which some life, yet unspent, might explode as it lay burning on the ground, is another matter; so are the ghosts, the ghostly echoes on paper, the repetition of salutes.

This, in fact, is the one poem of Thomas's whose subject-matter is poetical self-criticism. The poet is pondering whether he ought to make a bonfire—accompanied by small fireworks, perhaps dangerous ones—of childish fears, obsessions, and superstitions; a bonfire, also, in his writing of poetry of 'given' phrases, lines, and images—'ghostly echoes on paper'—about whose source and meaning he is not clear. He is wondering whether he ought to become, like so many of his contemporaries of the 1930s, an 'adult' and 'socially conscious' poet. He decides that he cannot afford to make this bonfire for the reason that the poetic lie, the undue fearsomeness and rhetoric—the 'ghosts' and the 'repetition of salutes'—are somehow bound up with the possibility of the full, life-giving poetic vision. The old lie, exploding, might leave him half-blind; the terrors from which he wants to move away are somehow inextricably linked with an image full of peace, dignity and beauty:

> ... as the day
> Goes over the hill into the deep sea.

I have been trying here to follow Mr Robert Graves's ideal technique of making a poem's drift clear by expounding it, at greater length, mainly in its own words. If the reader agrees with me about the poem's drift, he will admire the insight into his own poetic scope which Thomas shows in this poem. He was right to take the risk of regressiveness, rather than cut the tangle of links that bound him with his childhood; the obsession with childhood, even with its fictions and fantasies, was to lead him in the end to a rediscovery of innocence.

The most important and most obscure poems in *Twenty-five Poems* are, however, the ten sonnets beginning 'Altarwise by owl-light'. Mr Elder Olson has argued very persuasively that these sonnets evoke in succession pagan despair, the new hope consequent upon the birth of Christ, the Christian despair consequent upon the Crucifixion, and the renewed Christian hope consequent upon the Resurrection; very ingeniously, but perhaps a little less persuasively, he has suggested that these ideas are expressed through an almost pedantically exact symbolism drawn from the movements of the constellation Hercules, standing both for man, and for the manhood of Christ. For other readers, the sonnets had always seemed the most baffling of Dylan Thomas's works, though to a sympathetic reader the Christian overtones and the occasional presence of 'the grand style' were obvious from the start. There are fragments in these sonnets —which as whole remain, in Dr Daiches's phrases, oppressive and congested even after one has grasped and accepted the main lines of Mr Olson's exposition—more nobly eloquent than anything else Dylan Thomas ever wrote:

> This was the crucifixion on the mountain,
> Time's nerve in vinegar, the gallow grave
> As tarred with blood as the bright thorns I wept . . .
>
> Green as beginning, let the garden diving
> Soar, with its two black towers, to that Day
> When the worm builds with the gold straws of venom
> My nest of mercies in the rude, red tree.

The sonnets, a failure as a whole, splendid in such parts as these, are important because they announce the current of orthodox Christian feeling—feeling rather than thought—which was henceforth increasingly to dominate Thomas's work in poetry.

V. *THE MAP OF LOVE*

Thomas's third volume, *The Map of Love*, which contained prose pieces as well as poems, appeared in 1939, on the verge of the Second World War. It had a great and in many ways unfortunate influence on some of the younger English writers of that time, in particular on the movement called at first the New Apocalypse, and later, when it became a wider and even more shapeless stream of tendency, the New Romanticism. The prose pieces in *The Map of Love* were not at all like the straightforwardly descriptive and narrative, funny and pathetic pieces of *Portrait of the Artist as a Young Dog*, which came out in the following year, 1940. They were much influenced by the belated English interest in the French Surrealist and Dadaist movements. Mr David Gascoyne's excellent short book on Surrealism had appeared two or three years before *The Map of Love*, and more recently there had been Herbert Read's anthology of Surrealist texts and paintings published by Faber. The prose pieces in *The Map of Love* are not strictly Surrealist—they are too carefully worked over, as to their prose rhythms, and so on—but they have a semi-Surrealist flavour in their superficial incoherence, their reliance on shock tactics, and the cruelty or obscenity, or both, of much of their imagery. They are failures on the whole, artistically, but they have a real interest in relation to the total pattern of Thomas's work. They are his *pièces noires*, the pieces in which he accepts evil: they are one side of a medal of which the other side is Thomas's later celebration of innocence, and the benignity of the Reverend Eli Jenkins. In writing these pieces, Thomas was grappling with, and apparently succeeded in absorbing and overcoming, what Jungians call the Shadow.

Perhaps because of the comparative failure of these prose pieces, *The Map of Love* was the least popular of Thomas's volumes. It cannot have been printed in large numbers, or have gone into many impressions, for it is almost impossible—where with the other volumes it is fairly easy—

to procure a second-hand copy of it. Yet it contains some of Thomas's most memorable poems, chief among them the elegy 'After the Funeral' for his elderly cousin, Ann Jones. This is a piece of baroque eloquence: in the poet's own words,

> . . . this for her is a monstrous image blindly
> Magnified out of praise . . .

There are, however, three or four lines towards the end which transcend the baroque manner and which rank with the passages already quoted from the sonnets as among Thomas's finest isolated fragments.

Their appeal is simple, human, and direct:

> I know her scrubbed and sour humble hands
> Lie with religion in their cramp, her threadbare
> Whisper in a damp word, her wits drilled hollow,
> Her fist of a face died clenched on a round pain;
> And sculptured Ann is seventy years of stone.

Other, slighter poems in *The Map of Love* have interest as explorations of new aptitudes. A slight but charming poem, 'Once it was the colour of saying', gives a foretaste of one of Thomas's main later themes, the reminiscent celebration, through the evoking of a landscape that the perspective of time has made legendary, of childish innocence:

> Once it was the colour of saying
> Soaked my table the uglier side of a hill
> With a capsized field where a school sat still
> And a black and white patch of girls grew playing . . .
> The gentle seasides of saying I must undo
> That all the charmingly drowned arise to cockcrow and kill.
> When I whistled with mitching boys through a reservoir park
> Where at night we stoned the cold and cuckoo
> Lovers in the dirt of their leafy beds,
> The shade of their trees was a word of many shades
> And a lamp of lightning for the poor in the dark;
> Now my saying shall be my undoing,
> And every stone I wind off like a reel.

The 'capsized field' there—looking as if it had been upset or overturned on the hillside and also, from the distance, just the size of a schoolboy's cap—is a delightful example of the subdued punning which a careful reader of Thomas soon learns to look for everywhere. Yet even as late as 1939, Thomas's voice was still not always quite his own. Or rather, he had his own voice, but he would still from time to time try on other people's to see how they fitted. Asked, for instance, who was the author of the following stanza from *The Map of Love* an intelligent reader might well name Mr C. Day Lewis or Mr W. H. Auden. The turn and the mood of the last two lines, in particular, suggests that preoccupation of most of the poets of the 1930s with harsh historical necessity, which Dylan Thomas on the whole did not share:

> Bound by a sovereign strip, we lie,
> Watch yellow, wish for wind to blow away
> The strata of the shore and drown red rock;
> But wishes breed not, neither
> Can we fend off rock arrival . . .

It was biological necessity, rather, that preoccupied Thomas. That comes out in the last poem in this volume, flatly melancholy in its tone, but displaying a gift, new and unexpected in Thomas, for the forceful gnomic statement:

> Twenty-four years remind the tears of my eyes.
> (Bury the dead for fear that they walk to the grave in labour.)
> In the groin of the natural doorway I crouched like a tailor
> Sewing a shroud for a journey
> By the light of the meat-eating sun.
> Dressed to die, the sensual strut begun,
> With my red veins full of money,
> In the final direction of the elementary town
> I advance for as long as forever is.

VI. *DEATHS AND ENTRANCES* AND LATER POEMS

Among many critics of Thomas, there has been a tendency to attempt to enclose him within a formula; that of the man-nature equation used here to throw light on *Eighteen Poems*; that of adolescent sexual excitement used here for the same purpose; that of the religious celebrator of natural process; that of the disorderly breeder of images, struggling from sleep to wakefulness, and so on. There has been no general agreement about which formula is right, but there has been a general agreement that some formula would be, and also that there is a remarkable similarity about all Thomas's poems. I have been trying, in this sketch, to deal with each volume of Thomas's in turn, almost as if I had been reviewing it when it first came out. I hope I have conveyed my impression—an impression which, when it first came solidly home, very much surprised me—that in tone, in style, in subject matter Thomas is a much more various, a much less narrowly consistent poet, and that in attitude to life he is much more a developing poet, than people make him out to be. In *Eighteen Poems*, for instance, there is, in the ordinary senses of these words, no human or religious interest; the sonnets, at least, in *Twenty-five Poems* have a remarkable religious interest; and 'After the Funeral' and some other poems in *The Map of Love* have a human interest that is new.

Thomas was found unfit for military service and spent most of the years of the Second World War in Wales, coming up to London from time to time to see friends, do broadcasting work, or meet publishers. He never tackled the war directly as a subject, but at least two of his poems, the obscure but powerful title poem of *Deaths and Entrances* and the famous 'A Refusal to Mourn' have, for background, the bombing raids on London. I have been told that some work he did on a documentary film on the bombing raids, which in the end was found too grim for public release, had

a profound effect on his imagination; an effect that may
partly explain the retreat, in many of his later poems, to the
themes of childhood innocence and country peace. Certainly, in these years, Thomas did more and more tend to
turn, for the central themes of his poetry, to his Welsh
childhood. The same episodes which, in *Portrait of the Artist
as a Young Dog*, had provided material for comedy, now,
more deeply explored, brought forth a transformation of
memory into vision; a vision of a lost paradise regained.

Thomas's last English volume of new poems, *Deaths and
Entrances*, came out in 1946. It increases the impression of
variety, and of steady development, which the earlier
volumes, read in the order of their appearance, give. It contains a remarkable number of successful poems of notably
different kinds. One kind, in particular, at once caught the
fancy of a wide public. It is a kind which, very roughly,
throwing out words at a venture, one might call the recap-
tured-childish-landscape, semi-fairy-tale, semi-ode kind:
more concisely, the long poem of formal celebration. Such,
for instance, are seven late poems by Thomas: 'Poem in
October', 'A Winter's Tale', 'Fern Hill', 'In Country Sleep',
'Over Sir John's Hill', 'Poem on His Birthday', 'In the
White Giant's Thigh'. All these poems have a larger and
looser, a more immediately apprehensible rhythmical
movement than most of Thomas's earlier work. They do
not aim at dark, packed, and concentrated, but at bright,
expansive effects. Their landscapes are always partly magical
landscapes. Their common flavour can, however, perhaps
be better conveyed by a series of quotations than by such
remarks:

> Bird, he was brought low,
> Burning in the bride bed of love, in the whirl-
> Pool at the wanting centre, in the folds
> Of paradise, in the spun bud of the world.
> And she rose with him flowering in her melting snow . . .
>
> ('A Winter's Tale')

It was my thirtieth year to heaven
Woke to my hearing from harbour and neighbour wood
And the mussel pooled and heron
Priested shore
The morning beckon
With water praying and call of seagull and rook
And the knock of sailing boats on the net webbed wall
Myself to set foot
That second
In the still sleeping town and set forth . . .

('Poem in October')

I hear the bouncing hills
Grow larked and greener at berry brown
Fall and the dew lark sing
Taller this thunderclap spring, and how
More spanned with angels rise
The mansouled fiery islands; Oh
Holier then their eyes,
And my shining men no more alone
As I sail out to die . . .

('Poem on His Birthday')

Now as I was young and easy under the apple boughs
About the lilting house and happy as the grass was green,
The night above the dingle starry,
Time let me hail and climb
Golden in the heydays of his eyes,
And honoured among wagons I was prince of the apple towns
And once below a time I lordly had the trees and leaves
Trail with daisies and barley
Down the rivers of the windfall light.

('Fern Hill')

The dust of their kettles and clocks swings to and fro
Where the hay rides now or the bracken kitchens rust
As the arc of the billhooks that flashed the hedges low
And cut the birds' boughs that the minstrel sap ran red.
They from the houses where the harvest kneels, hold me hard,
Who heard from the tall bell sail down the Sundays of the dead
And the rain wring out its tongues on the faded years,

Teach me the love that is evergreen after the fall leaved
Grave, after the Belovéd on the grass gulfed cross is scrubbed
Off by the sun and Daughters no longer grieved
Save by their long desires in the fox cubbed
Streets or hungering in the crumbled wood: to these
Hale dead and deathless do the women of the hill
Love for ever meridian through the courters' trees

And the daughters of darkness flame like Fawkes fires still.
                              ('In the White Giant's Thigh')

Neither the style nor the mood of these passages would
have been easily predictable even by an exceptionally acute
critic of Dylan Thomas's earlier verse. The mood is close to
some of the verse of Vaughan and some of the prose of
Traherne, or to take a closer and more contemporary com-
parison from another art, there is something in this glowing
transformation of everyday things—a boy in an apple tree,
a young man going out for an early walk in a seaside town
on his birthday—that recalls some drawings by David Jones
or some paintings by Stanley Spencer. One would not,
with the same confidence, mention Wordsworth or Blake;
there is a kind of massiveness and sobriety in Wordsworth's
explorations of childish memory, there is a naked directness
in Blake's *Songs of Innocence*, that we do not find here.
Thomas, like Vaughan, Traherne, Spencer, or Jones, could
be described affectionately as 'quaint', his vision of paradise
as a 'touching' one; such epithets would be out of place if
one were discussing Blake or Wordsworth.

The style, also, has changed. Its main mark is no longer
an obscure concision, a dense packing of images, but a rapid
and muscular fluency that puts one in mind sometimes of a
more relaxed Hopkins, sometimes of a more concentrated
Swinburne. The tone of voice is a deliberately exalted one.
The seven poems I have mentioned, and some of which I
have quoted, are likely to remain Thomas's most popular
pieces. But for the special effect he is aiming at in them he
has eliminated that quality of cloudy pregnancy which,

rightly or wrongly, was for many readers one of the main fascinations of his earlier poems. It is not that these eloquent, sincere, and moving long poems are in any sense shallow; they make us gloriously free of a visionary world; yet there does remain a sense, if the Irishism is permissible, in which the depths are all on the surface. The poems give what they have to give, grandly, at once. One does not go back to them to prove and question. A passion for probing and questioning can, of course, vitiate taste. Yet there will always remain critics (by his own confession, Professor William Empson is one) to whom these lucid late successes are less 'interesting' than other late poems, more dense and obscure, much less certainly successful, but carrying the suggestion that, if they *were* successful, their success might be something higher still.

The quality that Thomas jettisoned in these late, long poems, rightly for his purposes, was a quality of dramatic compression. The title poem of *Deaths and Entrances* is, for instance, almost certainly on the whole a failure: if only for the reason that Thomas does not provide us with clues enough to find out what exactly is happening in the poem, and yet does provide us with clues enough to make us bother about what is happening. The setting is certainly the bombing raids on London:

> On almost the incendiary eve
>   Of several near deaths,
> When one at the great least of your best beloved
>   And always known must leave
> Lions and fires of his flying breath,
>   Of your immortal friends
> Who'd raise the organs of the counted dust
>   To shoot and sing your praise,
> One who called deepest down shall hold his peace
>   That cannot sink or cease
>   Endlessly to his wound
> In many married London's estranging grief.

To read that stanza is like seeing a man making a set of

noble gestures on a tragic stage and not quite catching, because of some failure of acoustics, what he is saying. Yet the gestures *are* noble, and I would claim that the last line in particular,

> In many married London's estranging grief,

is a fragmentary achievement of a kind of poetry higher in itself than the dingles and the apple boughs and the vale mist riding through the haygold stalls and even than the very lovely heron-priested shore; a kind of poetry which grasps and drastically unifies an unimaginably complex set of inter-related pains. Such a line suggests the immanence in Thomas, in his last years, of a poetry of mature human awareness.

In *Deaths and Entrances* and among the rarer few poems written after it, there are some shorter pieces that similarly seem to reach out for a mature human awareness. Among them are the beautifully constructed 'The Conversation of Prayer', 'A Refusal to Mourn the Death, by Fire, of a Child in London' (of which Professor William Empson has given a masterly exposition); the two very short, which are also among Thomas's few very personal, poems, 'To Others than You' and 'In My Craft and Sullen Art'; the plangent *villanelle*, with its Yeatsian overtones, addressed by Thomas to his dying father, 'Do Not Go Gentle into That Good Night', of which the intended sequel, recently reassembled by Vernon Watkins from Thomas's working notes, would have been an even more striking poem; and with less certainty 'There Was a Saviour'.

One of these poems, 'The Conversation of Prayer', is worth looking at on the page as an example of Thomas's extraordinary virtuosity as a creator of textures. I have marked, in italics, the hidden rhymes:

> The conversation of *prayers* about to be *said*
> By the child going to *bed* and the man on the *stairs*
> who climbs to his dying *love* in her high *room*
> The one not caring to *whom* in his sleep he will *move*,
> And the other full of *tears* that she will be *dead*,

Turns in the dark on the *sound* they know will *arise*
Into the answering *skies* from the green *ground*,
From the man on the *stairs* and the child by his *bed*.
The sound about to be *said* in the two *prayers*
For sleep in a safe *land* and the love who *dies*

Will be the same grief *flying*. Whom shall they calm?
Shall the child sleep un*harmed* or the man be *crying*?
The conversation of *prayers* about to be *said*
Turns on the quick and the *dead*, and the man on the *stairs*
Tonight shall find no *dying* but alive and *warm*

In the fire of his *care* his love in the high *room*.
And the child not caring to *whom* he climbs his *prayer*
Shall drown in a grief as *deep* as his true *grave*,
And mark the dark eyed *wave*, through the eyes of *sleep*,
Dragging him up the *stairs* to one who lies *dead*.

Apart from the extraordinary complexity of this rhyme scheme, the reader should notice that the vast majority of the words in the poem, most of the exceptions being participles, are monosyllables. The only word that is more than a disyllable is 'conversation' and it is also the most abstract word in the poem and the word that, as it were, states the poet's theme. No doubt any skilful craftsman might invent and carry through a form like this as a metrical exercise. But Thomas's poem does not read at all like an exercise; most readers, in fact, do not notice the rhyme-scheme till it is pointed out to them. Again, most poets would find it hard to construct a series of stanzas mainly in monosyllables without giving an effect of monotony. Thomas's line is so subtly varied as to defy an attempt at rule-of-thumb scansion. It is a four-stress line, with feet freely substituted, and in one case the four feet are four anapaests but with a dragging effect, because of their setting, that anapaests do not usually have:

For the *man*/on the *stairs*/and the *child*/by his *bed*.

Usually, however, the effect is far more subtle:

Who *climbs*/to his *dy*/ing *love*/in/her/*high room*.

There we have an iambus, an anapaest, an iambus and an unstressed two-syllable foot followed, according to English custom, by a two-stress foot. And that, to be sure, seems to make *five* stresses; but because 'high' chimes loudly with the first syllable of 'dying', earlier in the line, the word 'room' has actually only a secondary stress. Such minutiae are dry reading except for the teacher of metrics, but since Thomas has been accused by some critics, such as Mr Geoffrey Grigson, of careless and slapdash writing it is worth providing an almost mechanical demonstration of his mastery of his craft.

Yet the craft exists only for the sake of the art. 'The Conversation of Prayer', perhaps one of the most perfect of Thomas's short poems, may have been neglected because the idea around which it moves is, at least in Protestant countries, becoming marginal to our culture. It is the idea of the reversibility of grace; the idea that all prayers and all good acts co-operate for the benefit of all men, and that God, in His inscrutable mercy, can give the innocent the privilege of suffering some of the tribulations which have been incurred by redeemable sinners. The man in this poem might be the father of the boy, or he might have no connection with him; or the man and the boy might be the same person at different stages of their life histories. Both pray, and there is a sense in which prayer is eternally heard. The boy prays for 'sleep unharmed', for a night undisturbed by bad dreams, and the man whose wife or lover is dying prays that she may be better. The prayers, as it were, cross in the air, the man is granted his wish, for one night at least the sick woman is happy and well again, but the sleeping boy has to endure all the man's nightmare of climbing up the stairs to discover the loved one dead. Only this idea makes sense of the poem. How, it may be asked, could Thomas, bred a Bible Protestant, and never interested in abstruse notions, have come across it, or worked it out for himself? Perhaps it is an idea that all men who really struggle with prayer do, at least implicitly, work out for themselves. For, though Thomas's attitude to life was, as he grew older, an increasingly religious, and in a broad sense an increasingly Christian one, he was certainly not a poet, like Eliot for instance, to whom dry theological and metaphysical speculations were, in themselves, poetically exciting. His world was not a conceptual world and his coherency is not a conceptual coherency. Across the page in the *Collected Poems* from 'The Conversation of Prayer' there is the famous 'A Refusal to Mourn', whose drift Professor Empson has summed up as 'a pantheistic pessimism'. Thomas's longest personal religious poem, 'Vision and Prayer', offers us a naked confrontation of the desire for utter extinction with the hope of personal salvation. The last line of 'A Refusal to Mourn',

> After the first death, there is no other,

has a resonance and authority both for unbelievers and believers. At one level, the meaning may be, as Professor Empson suggests, that life is a cruel thing and that the utter finality of physical death is welcome; but the logically contradictory Christian overtones—'Do not let us fear death, since, once the body is dead, the soul lives for ever'—cannot possibly be excluded. We must respect the baffling simplicity of Thomas's unitary response and not impose abstract categories on him.

One poem in *Deaths and Entrances*, 'The Hunchback in the Park', a more descriptive and 'realistic' poem than Thomas was in the habit of writing, may help us, perhaps, to grasp this simplicity by watching it operate at a less profound level. This begins with a long but not obscure two-stanza sentence:

> The hunchback in the park
> A solitary mister
> Propped between trees and water
> From the opening of the garden lock
> That lets the trees and water enter
> Until the Sunday sombre bell at dark

Eating bread from a newspaper
Drinking water from the chained cup
That the children filled with gravel
In the fountain basin where I sailed my ship
Slept at night in a dog kennel
But nobody chained him up . . .

The boys in the park, of whom Thomas is one, mock and torment the solitary hunchback who, ignoring them, seeks happiness in a dream in which the park stands for all the richness of life from which he is locked out; and the boys are locked out from the poetic understanding of that richness which the hunchback has attained to through deprivation and pain. They are part of the richness, and how should they understand it (that may be part of the implication of the phrase, 'the wild boys innocent as strawberries', which several critics have found sentimental)? Hunter and hunted; mocked and mocker; boys and hunchback; growth and decay, life and death, dream and reality: all sets of polar opposites are, for Thomas, at some level equally holy and necessary, holy is the hawk, holy is the dove. . . . This theme, the coincidence of opposites, runs through all Thomas's work and the end of this poem states it clearly: how the hunchback, the 'old dog sleeper'

Made all day until bell time
A woman figure without fault
Straight as a young elm
Straight and tall from his crooked bones
That she might stand in the night
After the lock and chains

All night in the unmade park
After the railings and shrubberies
The birds the grass the trees the lake
And the wild boys innocent as strawberries
Had followed the hunchback
To his kennel in the dark.

Other poems in *Deaths and Entrances* show Thomas experimenting along still other lines. 'Ballad of the Long-Legged Bait' is his only poem, with the partial exception of 'A Winter's Tale', of which the movement is primarily a narrative one. It is a phantasmagoric narrative like Rimbaud's *Bâteau Ivre*. Its immediate impact is extremely confusing. Mr Elder Olson has worked out a logical structure for it. The poet goes fishing in a magic boat, using a naked woman for a bait, and all the sea creatures eat her up, and then as in the Book of Revelations 'there is no more sea'. She is a woman, and she is also his heart, and he has been sacrificing the desires of his heart to restore a lost Eden. In the end, Eden is restored, and so is the woman, and the heart in its lost innocence; the poet steps out of the boat, now on dry land and

> stands alone at the door of his home
> With his long-legged heart in his hand.

The poem, thus, for Mr Olson is a kind of small allegory about the struggle inside Thomas, a typically Welsh struggle, between natural sensuality and Puritan mysticism. Thomas himself, more modestly, over a bar in New York, said that the poem is about how a young man goes out fishing for fun and games, for all the excitements of the wild free life, and finds in the end that he has caught a wife, some children, and a little house. The poem, even with the help of these clues, remains unsatisfactory—it leaves one feeling a little sea-sick—but it is yet another example of Thomas's eagerness, throughout his poetic career, to go on extending his range. And as a whole *Deaths and Entrances* does remain one of the two or three most impressive single volumes of poetry published in English over the last twenty years.

VII. CONCLUSION

Let us now try to sum up. In the years immediately after his death, Dylan Thomas's reputation as a poet undoubtedly suffered at least a mild slump. He was always far too directly and massively an emotional poet, and in the detail of his language often too confusing and sometimes apparently confused a poet, to be acceptable to the poets and critics of the so-called 'Movement' school, like Mr Philip Larkin, or Mr John Wain, who began to become prominent soon after Thomas's death. Quite apart from that, there is quite generally in literary history a time lag, sometimes of as long as twenty or thirty years, between a notable writer's death and the attempt to reach a balanced judgement on him. The difficulty, also, at least at the level of attempting to explain in prose what the poet is doing, of Dylan Thomas's work has meant that most of the books about him—by, among others, Mr Henry Treece, Mr Elder Olson, Mr Derek Stanford, Mr Clark Emery, Mr T. H. Jones, Mr H. H. Kleinman, Mr William York Tindall, Mr Ralph Maud— have been expository rather than critical. Mr Stanford thinks he may rank in English literary history rather as Gray ranks; this may be too high an estimate, for where is Thomas's long poem of mature moral interest, where is his 'Elegy Written in a Country Churchyard'? But he might well rank as Collins ranks; he has written some perfect poems, his poetic personality is a completely individual one, he brings in a new note. One might call Gray a minor major poet; one might call Collins a major minor poet. That, possibly, is also Thomas's rank, but at the same time we should be profoundly suspicious of this classroom, or examination-school, attitude to poets. There is a very real and profound sense in which poets do not compete with each other. No true poet offers us something for which anything else, by any other true poet, is really a substitute. It is enough, for the purposes here, to insist that Thomas was a good poet and worth our attention; and to attempt to define, and make vivid, his specific quality.

The reaction against Thomas, since his death, has, in fact, really been concerned to deny that Thomas was a good poet; or to assert that he might have been a good poet, but cheated poetically, in a way that disqualifies him. Thus, Mr John Wain has remarked that a meaning, or a set of meanings, can nearly always be got out of Thomas's poems but that the critic's worry is whether Thomas ever cared much what the meanings were so long as the thing sounded all right. Even more sharply, in his witty and provocative Clark Lectures, *The Crowning Privilege*, Mr Robert Graves condemns Thomas as a poet who takes care of the sound and lets the sense take care of itself: Mr Graves compares Thomas to a soldier firing off a rifle at random while a confederate in the butts—the confederate being the gullible reviewer of contemporary poetry—keeps on signalling bulls and inners, whether or not the bullet has come anywhere near the target.

How much justice is there in such strictures? There are certainly poems by Dylan Thomas of which many readers must find even the main drift, as sense, hard to grasp; there is hardly any poem of Thomas's of which some details, at least, are not likely to puzzle most readers. But I hope I have shown two things: that in Thomas's best poems there is a coherent meaning, and that it is not always mechanically the same meaning. It is simply not true that he went on writing, with variations of form and imagery, the same archetypal poem over and over again; he grew and changed and at his death was still developing, in the direction of a wider and more genial human scope. The importance of *Under Milk Wood* is that it shows him, at the very end of his life, transforming into a kind of poetry that humorous apprehension of life which, in *Portrait of the Artist as a Young Dog*, is still something quite separate from poetry. Had he lived, he might have worked into his poetry the shrewdness and the gaiety that make him a first-rate prose entertainer. His feeling for life, at the end, was growing, not shrinking; and the separated elements of it, the outer and the inner being, the legendary sweet funny man and the fine solemn poet, were growing together.

Ten years after Dylan Thomas's death, both that temporary cooling of the critical temperature which often follows the passing away of a notable writer and the reaction of shocked puritanism which followed the revelation, by his friend Mr Brinnin and by his widow, of some of the sadder and untidier aspects of Thomas's life have had time to die away. The individuality and distinction of his poetry, the dedicated craftsmanship behind it, are perhaps more apparent now that Thomas has no longer, as in his lifetime, a crowd of minor imitators and now that most of these imitators are themselves forgotten. Thomas has not been helped, perhaps, by an anxiety on the part of some of his admirers to prove that *all* his poems can be paraphrased satisfactorily in prose—these prose paraphrases, not having the advantage of any cohesion of rhythm and diction, are often more puzzling than the original poems themselves—and that many of them contain recondite and remote allusions, rather like those in T. S. Eliot's *The Waste Land* or *Ash Wednesday*; it would be a mistake to under-estimate the range of Thomas's reading, or the amount of material which he, like other poets, could absorb from even rapid and casual reading, but he was certainly not a learned or scholarly poet in Eliot's sense. His poems move us, in spite of their obscurity, because they deal with very immediate and intimate feelings; one impulse behind them, perhaps a main impulse, was towards an intricate and coherent patterning of words, rhythms, and images; and of all recent critics, Professor Ralph Maud, in his insistence on taking the poems as self-contained poetic enactments—as containing in their own antitheses and resolutions the best clue to proper poetic understanding—is probably, in his book, *Entrances to Dylan Thomas's Poetry*, most on the right track.

Let me end this sketch by quoting a short, very personal poem of Thomas's which warns us wholesomely against the kind of undue familiarity to which his public legend, the memory of his personality, the critic's dangerous passion for summary judgements, might all invite us:

TO OTHERS THAN YOU

Friend by enemy I call you out.

You with a bad coin in your socket,
You my friend there with a winning air
Who palmed the lie on me when you looked
Brassily at my shyest secret,
Enticed with twinkling bits of the eye
Till the sweet tooth of my love bit dry,
Rasped at last, and I stumbled and sucked,
Whom I now conjure to stand as a thief
In the memory worked by mirrors,
With unforgettably smiling act,
Quickness of hand in the velvet glove
And my whole heart under your hammer,
Were once such a creature, so gay and frank
A desireless familiar
I never thought to utter and think
While you displaced a truth in the air,

That though I loved them for their faults
As much as for their good,
My friends were enemies on stilts,
With their heads in a cunning cloud.

I hope that the truths displaced in the air in these pages have
been displaced towards their proper locations; I hope that in
all I have been saying my head, too, has not been in a
cunning cloud. I remember Dylan Thomas's own head,
benignly calm, as it looked in a photograph of his death-
mask which a close friend of his, the poet Ruthven Todd,
brought to show to Thomas's friends in London: it should
have made me think of two lines of Thomas's, not well
known:

And when blind sleep drops on the spying senses,
The heart is sensual, though five eyes break.

DYLAN THOMAS

A Select Bibliography

(Place of publication London, unless stated otherwise)

Bibliography:

DYLAN THOMAS: A Bibliography, by J. A. Rolph (1956).

Collected and Selected Works:

THE WORLD I BREATHE; Norfolk, Conn. (1939)
—a limited edition of 700 copies.

SELECTED WRITINGS, Introduction by J. L. Sweeney; Norfolk, Conn. (1946).

COLLECTED POEMS, 1934–1952 (1952).

A PROSPECT OF THE SEA AND OTHER STORIES AND PROSE WRITINGS, ed. D. Jones (1955).

THE LETTERS OF DYLAN THOMAS TO VERNON WATKINS (1957).

Separate Works:

18 POEMS (1934).

TWENTY-FIVE POEMS (1936).

THE MAP OF LOVE (1939). *Verse and Prose*

PORTRAIT OF THE ARTIST AS A YOUNG DOG (1940). *Stories*

NEW POEMS; Norfolk, Conn. (1943).

DEATHS AND ENTRANCES (1946). *Verse*

TWENTY-SIX POEMS (1950)
—a limited edition of 150 copies, signed by the author, printed at the Officina Bodoni, Verona. Only 50 copies were for sale in Great Britain, the rest being distributed in the USA by New Directions.

IN COUNTRY SLEEP; Norfolk, Conn. (1952)
—contains only six poems.

THE DOCTOR AND THE DEVILS: From the story by Donald Taylor (1953). *Film Scenario*

UNDER MILK WOOD: A Play for Voices (1954). *Prose*
—published posthumously. (An earlier and shorter draft appeared in Marguerite Caetani's *Botteghe Oscure*.)

QUITE EARLY ONE MORNING (1954). *Broadcasts*

ADVENTURES IN THE SKIN TRADE AND OTHER STORIES (1955).

THE BEACH OF FALESÁ (1964)
—film script based on Robert Louis Stevenson's story.

Note: A mock detective story, with skits on contemporary poets, written in collaboration with John Davenport, was announced for 1960, but never appeared.

Letters:

SELECTED LETTERS OF DYLAN THOMAS, ed. C. Fitzgibbon (1967).

Some Biographical and Critical Studies:

'The Explanation', by W. Empson, *Strand Magazine*, March 1947
—an exposition of 'A Refusal to Mourn'.

THE POETRY OF DYLAN THOMAS, by E. Olson; Chicago (1954).

DYLAN THOMAS: A LITERARY STUDY, by D. Stanford (1954).

DYLAN THOMAS IN AMERICA, by J. M. Brinnin (1955).

THE CROWNING PRIVILEGE, by R. Graves (1955)
—contains references to Thomas's work.

LITERARY ESSAYS, by D. Daiches (1956).

DYLAN THOMAS, DOG AMONG THE FAIRIES, by H. Treece (1956).

THE ROMANTIC SURVIVAL, by J. Bayley (1957).

LEFT OVER LIFE TO KILL, by C. Thomas (1957).

PRELIMINARY ESSAYS, by J. Wain (1957).

A GRAMMAR OF METAPHOR, by C. Brooke-Rose (1958).

VISION AND RHETORIC, by G. S. Fraser (1959).

LLAREGGUB REVISITED: DYLAN THOMAS AND THE STATE OF MODERN POETRY, by D. Holbrook (1962).

A READER'S GUIDE TO DYLAN THOMAS, by W. Y. Tindall (1962).

THE WORLD OF DYLAN THOMAS, by C. W. Emery; Coral Gables (1963).

DYLAN THOMAS, by T. H. Jones; Edinburgh (1963).

DYLAN THOMAS: HIS LIFE AND WORK, by J. Ackerman (1964).

DYLAN: DRUID OF THE BROKEN BODY, by A. T. Davies (1964).

THE RELIGIOUS SONNETS OF DYLAN THOMAS, by H. H. Kleinman (1964).

ENTRANCES TO DYLAN THOMAS'S POETRY, by R. Maud (1964).

THE LIFE OF DYLAN THOMAS, by C. Fitzgibbon (1965)
—the definitive biography.

WRITERS AND THEIR WORK

CLOUGH: Isobel Armstrong
COLERIDGE: Kathleen Raine
CREEVEY & GREVILLE: J. Richardson
DE QUINCEY: Hugh Sykes Davies
DICKENS: K. J. Fielding
   EARLY NOVELS: T. Blount
   LATER NOVELS: B. Hardy
DISRAELI: Paul Bloomfield
GEORGE ELIOT: Lettice Cooper
FERRIER & GALT: W. M. Parker
FITZGERALD: Joanna Richardson
MRS GASKELL: Miriam Allott
GISSING: A. C. Ward
THOMAS HARDY: R. A. Scott-James
          and C. Day Lewis
HAZLITT: J. B. Priestley
HOOD: Laurence Brander
G. M. HOPKINS: Geoffrey Grigson
T. H. HUXLEY: William Irvine
KEATS: Edmund Blunden
LAMB: Edmund Blunden
LANDOR: G. Rostrevor Hamilton
EDWARD LEAR: Joanna Richardson
MACAULAY: G. R. Potter
MEREDITH: Phyllis Bartlett
JOHN STUART MILL: M. Cranston
WILLIAM MORRIS: P. Henderson
NEWMAN: J. M. Cameron
PATER: Iain Fletcher
PEACOCK: J. I. M. Stewart
ROSSETTI: Oswald Doughty
CHRISTINA ROSSETTI: G. Battiscombe
RUSKIN: Peter Quennell
SIR WALTER SCOTT: Ian Jack
SHELLEY: Stephen Spender
SOUTHEY: Geoffrey Carnall
R. L. STEVENSON: G. B. Stern
SWINBURNE: H. J. C. Grierson
TENNYSON: F. L. Lucas
THACKERAY: Laurence Brander
FRANCIS THOMPSON: P. Butter
TROLLOPE: Hugh Sykes Davies
OSCAR WILDE: James Laver
WORDSWORTH: Helen Darbishire

Twentieth Century:
CHINUA ACHEBE: A. Ravenscroft
W. H. AUDEN: Richard Hoggart
HILAIRE BELLOC: Renée Haynes
ARNOLD BENNETT: F. Swinnerton
EDMUND BLUNDEN: Alec M. Hardie
ELIZABETH BOWEN: Jocelyn Brooke
ROBERT BRIDGES: J. Sparrow
ROY CAMPBELL: David Wright
JOYCE CARY: Walter Allen
G. K. CHESTERTON: C. Hollis
WINSTON CHURCHILL: John Connell
R. G. COLLINGWOOD: E. W. F. Tomlin
I. COMPTON-BURNETT: P. H. Johnson

JOSEPH CONRAD: Oliver Warner
WALTER DE LA MARE: K. Hopkins
NORMAN DOUGLAS: Ian Greenlees
T. S. ELIOT: M. C. Bradbrook
FIRBANK & BETJEMAN: J. Brooke
FORD MADOX FORD: Kenneth Young
E. M. FORSTER: Rex Warner
CHRISTOPHER FRY: Derek Stanford
JOHN GALSWORTHY: R. H. Mottram
WM. GOLDING: Clive Pemberton
ROBERT GRAVES: M. Seymour-Smith
GRAHAM GREENE: Francis Wyndham
L. P. HARTLEY & ANTHONY POWELL:
    P. Bloomfield and B. Bergonzi
A. E. HOUSMAN: Ian Scott-Kilvert
ALDOUS HUXLEY: Jocelyn Brooke
HENRY JAMES: Michael Swan
PAMELA HANSFORD JOHNSON:
            Isabel Quigly
JAMES JOYCE: J. I. M. Stewart
RUDYARD KIPLING: Bonamy Dobrée
D. H. LAWRENCE: Kenneth Young
C. DAY LEWIS: Clifford Dyment
WYNDHAM LEWIS: E. W. F. Tomlin
COMPTON MACKENZIE: K. Young
LOUIS MACNEICE: John Press
KATHERINE MANSFIELD: Ian Gordon
JOHN MASEFIELD: L. A. G. Strong
SOMERSET MAUGHAM: J. Brophy
GEORGE MOORE: A. Norman Jeffares
EDWIN MUIR: J. C. Hall
J. MIDDLETON MURRY: Philip Mairet
SEAN O'CASEY: W. A. Armstrong
GEORGE ORWELL: Tom Hopkinson
POETS OF 1939-45 WAR: R. N. Currey
POWYS BROTHERS: R. C. Churchill
J. B. PRIESTLEY: Ivor Brown
HERBERT READ: Francis Berry
FOUR REALIST NOVELISTS: V. Brome
BERNARD SHAW: A. C. Ward
EDITH SITWELL: John Lehmann
OSBERT SITWELL: Roger Fulford
KENNETH SLESSOR: C. Semmler
C. P. SNOW: William Cooper
STRACHEY: R. A. Scott-James
SYNGE & LADY GREGORY: E. Coxhead
DYLAN THOMAS: G. S. Fraser
EDWARD THOMAS: Vernon Scannell
G. M. TREVELYAN: J. H. Plumb
WAR POETS: 1914-18: E. Blunden
EVELYN WAUGH: Christopher Hollis
H. G. WELLS: Montgomery Belgion
PATRICK WHITE: R. F. Brissenden
CHARLES WILLIAMS: J. Heath-Stubbs
ANGUS WILSON: K. W. Gransden
VIRGINIA WOOLF: B. Blackstone
W. B. YEATS: G. S. Fraser
ANDREW YOUNG & R. S. THOMAS:
    L. Clark and R. G. Thomas

A22959

PR6039
H52Z4
1964

Fraser, George Sutherland, 1915-
    Dylan Thomas. [Rev. ed.   London] Published
for the British Council and the National Book
League by Longmans [c1964]
    40 p.   port. (Bibliographical series of sup
plements to British book news on writers and
their work)

    1. Thomas, Dylan, 1914-1953.